Furniture

Lorraine Mariner was born in 1974, grew up in Upminster and attended Huddersfield University, where she read English, and University College London, where she read Library and Information Studies. She works at the Poetry Library, Southbank Centre. Her pamphlet 'Bye For Now' was published by *The Rialto* in 2005. In 2005 she also received an Arts Council Writer's Award and in 2007 her poem 'Thursday' was shortlisted for the Forward Prize for best individual poem.

Furniture

Lorraine Mariner

PICADOR

First published 2009 by Picador
an imprint of Pan Macmillan Ltd
Pan Macmillan, 20 New Wharf Road, London N1 9RR
Basingstoke and Oxford
Associated companies throughout the world
www.panmacmillan.com

ISBN 978-0-330-45825-2

9 8 7 6 5 4 3 2 1

A CIP catalogue record for this book is available from
the British Library.

Printed and bound in the UK by
CPI Mackays, Chatham ME5 8TD

For Chris, Gemma and Lydia

Acknowledgements are due to the editors of the following publications, in which some of these poems have appeared: *Connect, Dripping, The Forward Book of Poetry 2008, I Am Twenty People: a Third Anthology from The Poetry School, Limelight, Magma, Mslexia, Other Poetry, Skein of Geese: Poems from the 100 Poets Gathering at StAnza 2007, Smiths Knoll, Soundings, The Interpreter's House, The Rialto.*

Some of these poems were published in the pamphlet 'Bye For Now', *The Rialto*, 2005.

Special thanks to Michael Mackmin, Dean Parkin, Don Paterson, Carole Satyamurti, Siriol Troup and my colleagues at the Poetry Library, Southbank Centre. Thanks also to Finuala Dowling who introduced me to Jessica Elton.

Contents

Furniture

Stanley

Yesterday evening I finished
with my imaginary boyfriend.
He knew what I was going to say
before I said it which was top of my list
of reasons why we should end it.

My other reasons were as follows:
he always does exactly what I tell him;
nothing in our relationship has ever surprised me;
he has no second name.

He took it very well
all things considered.
He told me I was to think of him
as a friend and if I ever need him
I know where he is.

Assertiveness role play

I am your work colleague, neighbour and friend.
I have a dog. I'm always going away for the weekend
and expect you to look after my dog which means
you can't go anywhere. You've had enough.
I say *Hi Michael. How are you?* You say *Fine.*
I say *I'm off to Rome.* You say *That's nice.*
I say *I'll drop Rover round on Friday.* You say *No*
and use your "broken record"; *Lorraine, I'm sorry,*
I'm not going to look after your dog any more.
I want to be free at the weekend. I'm supposed to
keep asking and you're supposed to keep saying
I'm not going to look after your dog again
but instead you touch my leg and say *Ok*
bring round your dog. How can I refuse you?
The trainer is not impressed. She doesn't think
you're taking this course seriously. The other pairs
are still in role so we have time to kill and I ask you
if you like dogs but you don't because of a stupid
Afghan Hound you had as a child, while the part of me
deep inside that knows what it wants says
Forget my dog. He's a figment of the trainer's imagination.
You are not. I noticed when we had to share one thing
we like to do at the start of the course, yours was going
to an Italian class. Well, I'm learning the language too
only I didn't like to say in case you thought
I was making it up but . . . vieni a Roma con me.
This will be my broken record; *Come with me to Rome.*
I've never been and the ice cream I'm planning to eat
on the Spanish Steps is too big for one. To show
that we mean business the trainer says we need a limit,

something that we will do if our needs don't seem
to be getting met. Not an empty threat. What you say
you have to carry through. *Michael, come with me to Italy
or my dog will bite you. Or I will.* My bottom line.

What percentage of the world's water is contained in a cow?

Ms Elton and her colleagues
are surprised by the question
but are not deterred.
Firstly, to how many decimal points
do they want their answer?
Secondly, what type of cow
are we talking here
and in which part of the world
would we find it? And the farmer,
is he generous with his feed?
Is he organic? Jessica Elton looks square
into the entrance examiner's eyes
and takes a sip from her glass.

Chair

The staff room where I used to sit has a chair in it,
different from all the other chairs, where my boss always sat.
The chair was there before she came; it wasn't her chair,
but she always sat in it and the rest of us never sat in it,
even when she wasn't there, because it had become her chair.

Of the other chairs, I often found myself drawn to one
that looked out of the window, but when I noticed my boss
sitting in her same different chair each break time, I tried
to make myself sit in a different same chair and appreciate
the walls, and my career goal became, 'Never be chair-tied'.

If you read this and find yourself sitting in a staff room in a chair
you always sit in or which you feel you should sit in, turn and say
This is not my chair to the person sitting alongside you. Or if you
read this and find yourself looking at a chair you would like to sit in,
stand up and get out of there as quickly as you can.

Postmistress

My friends laughed when the computerised psychometric test
we took at school recommended I pursue a career
as a post office clerk, thinking of the battle-axe that sat
behind the counter of the post office we'd grown up with.
But at the post office this lunchtime there was something comforting
in the firm hand pressing ink stamp to paper; the air mail stickers
were bluer than any sky I'd ever seen and I could do worse
than find myself a sub post office to manage, where I could bestow
pensions and tax discs and at first light each morning
launch my very own fleet of postmen, the best sort of men,
the ones that know the only way to live this life is free in the afternoon.

Section 3 – Write text – p.22

Jessica Elton is learning how to text
predictively. She is also trying to work out
what sort of person these words
have been predicted for. A teenager?
But why *Book* before *Cool*?
A city trader? *Money* comes straight up
as do *Shares* but why *Sub* before *Pub*?
Perhaps venture capitalists rate football
above alcohol? However, Jessica's phone refuses
to swear and who on earth wants a *Nun*
before their *Mum*? Jessica Elton is puzzled
but she does know that when she exits
the underground and her phone beeps to inform her
that a new message has been received
her bag seems to become heavier.

My wedding

Since discovering that I am due to be married
at a church in Preston on the fifteenth of September

I have decided to never again type my name
into an Internet search engine. That she will soon

be someone else is some consolation, while the thought
of her reading one of my poems is not, knowing

the shock I felt on finding I was living in Lancashire
and had changed denomination for the sake of Trevor,

nor the thought that maybe we are living each other's lives
and she would make a better poet, I a better Methodist.

Bye for now

Your repeated use of this phrase
at the end of emails
convinced me that we had a future

until I noticed that BBC
newsreaders and weather forecasters
say it to sign themselves off

secure in the knowledge
that some percentage of the population
will still be there later on

even for the World Weatherview
at one o'clock in the morning
even if they're dead in their armchairs

waiting to be discovered by the neighbours.

Feathers

With the woman from your office that you left her for
away at a weekend conference, you found yourself
at a party staring at your ex-girlfriend and her
new boyfriend, and deciding that the new boyfriend's
jumper was the kind favoured by train spotters or
watchers of birds (the sort that fly without any help
from you) repaired to the bedroom set aside for coats,
got as close as you could to the dressing-table mirror,
and practised saying *For old times' sake* with your eyes.

But you didn't know that on the evenings you were
working late, she had put off going home to an empty flat
by browsing in a bookshop near the station, and read
in the poetry section that hope is the thing with feathers
and in the natural world section that ninety per cent
of bird species are monogamous compared with
three per cent of mammals, and bought herself a pocket
guide by Bill Oddie and binoculars one lunchtime from a
sports shop, and waited for the day when you would leave.

So when you approached her at the buffet table
your 'come to bed' look didn't register and you found
yourself demanding *Who's the fucking jumper?*

Refilling their glasses in the kitchen her new boyfriend
picked up that stunned silence in which he could have
told you about the day on Hackney Marsh
when from his hide he saw her walking towards him,
a new variety that he couldn't name, who wanted to learn
everything he could teach her and had him describe swans

mating for life again and again and again, and how much
she loves his jumpers, particularly this one,
bought by her and worn by him to repel birds of prey.

Littlewoods

Growing up, Jessica Elton longed to live
in her mother's Littlewoods catalogue.
It wasn't so much the endless supply
of carefully described toys
as the adults in the clothing section,
so calm in their freshly pressed coordinates,
pointing in what could only be the right direction.

My beast

When I was a child I worried
that when I got my chance to love a beast
I would not be up to the task.
As he came in for the kiss I'd turn away
or gag on the mane in my mouth.

But now I see that the last thing my father,
driving home late from work,
would have on his mind is the gardens flashing by
and he would never stop to pick a rose
for one of his daughters

and if some misfortune,
such as his Volvo reversing into a beast's carriage,
did occur and I ended up at the castle as compensation,
the beast would probably just set me to work cleaning
and I'd never look up from scrubbing a floor
and catch him in the doorway
admiring my technique.

Still, as I've heard my dad say,
he and his children may not always be brilliant
but we always turn up,
and in time when the beast comes to realise
that I haven't tried to escape
he'll give me leave one Sunday a month to visit my family
and access to his vast library

and in bed at night reading by the light of a candle
I'll shut another calf-bound volume
and listen to its quality thud
with something like happiness.

Injured

At school I always wanted to get injured.
To have crutches and a whole group of new friends
trailing me at playtime, or stitches, or a serious illness,
say diabetes (like my oldest friend Nicola's dad)
fussed over by the mother of a birthday party
with my own special plate of sugar-free finger food.
Like Katrina, who broke her arm one lunchtime
and was made to do PE that afternoon by her
unsympathetic teacher, who always had her favourites
and didn't believe her. When my forearm ached years later
it would have been a pleasure to remember the faces
of Mrs Hunt and her pets, as I came in the next day
with my father wanting a word and my plaster cast
like an exclamation mark, white against the blackboard.

Swimming lesson

I think it was Stuart, at the Upminster Windmill
standing beneath the slats of the wooden stairs
to look up the skirt of Michelle's mother
as she descended sideways in high-heeled sandals.
And I'm certain it was Stuart nudging me in class
to look down the cleavage of Miss Bowler
bent over us in her bold flowered summer dress
showing us how to do something I can't remember now.
And it must have been Stuart, holding on beside me
in Hornchurch swimming pool, which was how
I came to be looking up the shorts of our swimming instructor
while she stood on the side demonstrating
the correct way to move your legs during breaststroke.

That lesson was the kindest she'd ever been
possibly because of my wide-eyed expression
which she took to be some kind of miraculous conversion
to the joy of swimming, when what she could actually see
was terror as I caught glimpses, as her leg circled
above my head, of the result of abandoning depilation
following a career spent in swimsuits. What I could see
up there was my future, the one that came after Miss Bowler's
beautiful breasts. My leg action must have been perfect
as I breaststroked past the instructor later that morning,
trying to make amends for my betrayal, comprehending
another us and them apart from pupils and teachers,
and that I would never look again where Stuart was pointing.

Suntan

The last time Jessica Elton had a suntan
she was eleven years old. Over the summer holidays
her mother would lock her out of the house
after her cornflakes and wouldn't let her back in
until her father got home. Jessica then spent
the next six weeks with red-headed Ian Morrison
playing ball girl to his Boris Becker, assistant
to his Doctor Who, victim to his Jaws
at the swimming pool. When she turned twelve
Jessica discovered the bean bags at the public library
and Victorian novels. For three days, Ian stood baffled
outside the window of the children's section,
a sudden orphan, turning a dangerous shade of pink.

Mother Goose

The goose I wouldn't say boo to
has me locked in my bedroom,
is laying a wall of golden eggs
against the door.

The goose I wouldn't say boo to
pecks against the lintel
as I vow *I will try harder,*
I will be strong.

The goose I wouldn't say boo to
puts her eye to the keyhole when I do;
with a look which says
You made that bed

and there will never
be any feathers in it.

Say I forgot

Say I forgot how to love you, the way
when I was eight I forgot how to swim?
Could you steel yourself as my mother did
when she enrolled me in lessons for the holiday,
sat up in the stalls with a four-year-old
every morning for a month and afternoons
took me swimming herself in a learner pool
let me grip her hands willing me to let go?
I don't know what makes a child doubt
the water is able to keep her afloat,
think that the other side is too remote
but if I froze, could you wait it out
until I'm propelled again towards your smile
and wrapped tight in your towel like the first time?

The Bank of England

Whether the Bank of England will
they have been but still historically
there's no right answer.
Management points out that if
the cheapest fixes now
are going even further at
what to do with their mortgages
to be sure that their monthly repayments
might happen next and your ability.
This option isn't much use.

One more rise in the cost of
two years with an arrangement
the most effective option for
a short-term crisis like this would
if you're already stretched close.
Existing customers alike follow
to breaking point by the cost of
all of Britain's leading
stop even being aware that
the truth is no one really.

From an article by David Prosser
The Independent 27 Jan. 2007

London Lite

Some evenings Jessica Elton
feels she has been washed home
on a tide of free newspapers.
Getting on the tube after rush hour
the carriage is strewn with actresses
falling out of cars or relationships.
The reporters would have Jessica believe
that these women are drowning,
but how could they with those legs?

Elvis Presley

If as you foresee
I'm to become nothing more
than a caricature of myself

then I'm going down

not as a librarian
answering the phone
to hear somebody groan
I've called the library
and she's whispering

but in a white flared jumpsuit
mopping my brow
on a handkerchief
provided by a gorgeous woman
from the crowd
which she wants back

leaving my daughter my fortune.

From now on

my social life will be run
like a high-volume
burger and shake operation.
If you are not
at the designated place
five minutes
after your allotted time
I won't be waiting.
If you can't return my
texts/emails/calls
within forty-eight hours
(excepting immediate
family bereavement
and hospitalisation)
do not assume I'll
be in touch. Friends
like pieces of beef
are available
on every high street.
There'll be no seating
area in this franchise.

Shop names

It's Saturday and from her seat
on the upper deck of the number 52
Jessica Elton is collecting shop names.
Near the station she spots *Beddy Buys*.
Turning a corner there's a hairdressers
opening next week *Headonizm*
though she's sure it's no longer
cutting edge to replace an *s*
with a *z*. She hugs her handbag to her chest,
thinking of the promotional postcard it contains
for a champagne-tasting mini-break in Reims.
Grape Escapes.
Jessica Elton smiles. Indeed.

Furniture

The first you heard of someone acquiring furniture,
other than your parents, was a friend of yours
from university taking a day's leave to await
the delivery of a dining table. You thought her crazy;
wasn't annual leave for going to the beach?

It caught you unawares, your desire to acquire furniture,
you, who'd only ever known the fully-furnished,
the three white goods. But sitting with friends
on deck chairs in their living room, their new sofa
under construction, your heart sped up.

You received a photo in the post of furniture –
or rather your first friend to acquire a table
had acquired two blond boys tumbling
on a rug you'd seen in Habitat, in front of a nest
of tables, a rocking chair, a cabinet full of Portmeirion.

How had she managed to acquire so much furniture?
Both of you still in your twenties. Throat constricting
you wheeled in your shoe tidy, stroked the rack
holding your CDs, said out loud *Look, I have furniture!*
Promised yourself a table lamp and a trip out to the estuary.

There is nothing wrong with my sister

After you told my sister
that there was no one else
but you no longer wanted her,
she went to bed and tried to work out
what she had done
and what was wrong with her
and spent the night awake.

There is nothing wrong with my sister
but may there be something wrong
with the Ikea wardrobe
she helped you to build,
so that tonight it falls apart
and wakes you
from your unaccompanied sleep.

Many happy returns

It's her birthday and Jessica Elton
has taken her parents to a restaurant
she's always wanted to go to
in her lunch hour. Her father
is silently manoeuvring his way
through a plate of steamed cod,
topped with parmesan cheese,
specially prepared by the assistant
to the Michelin-starred chef. You see
in Jessica's family they don't talk
about what's troubling them; instead
they develop stomach complaints
and reintroduce controversial foods
back into their diets, one at a time.

Heart

Then there was the night leaving the pub
where she lost her heart by slipping it
into his pocket as he did up his overcoat.
On the bus going home he bruised it
when he sat on it, thinking *My seat seems
to be ticking?* When he found it,
feeling for his door key, it was still warm.
After sleeping with it on his bedside table
he placed it next to his computer at work
until his boss pointed out it was upsetting
the other members of staff; *No plants . . .*
In the evening he went back to the pub
to show the landlady, who pointed her out
slumped in the corner, blue in the face,
barely breathing, to which he said *Fancy,
giving your heart away so easily!* The landlady
agreed, so the kitchen staff cooked it,
and he ate it, with a pint of Guinness.

Adam

Testing the new filling in my mouth with my tongue
I'm walking to the station from the dentist's,
when the man who'd sat opposite me in the waiting room
pulls up in his car, guesses where I'm headed, offers me a lift.
Though he could be the father of any of my friends,
a serial granddad, I don't know him from Adam,
couldn't possibly say yes, but when I say no thanks
he seems so offended, puts his foot down as I quicken my steps.
Watching his tail lights disappear around the corner,
along with an earlier train to my job in the city,
I'm sorry it's not a September morning four hundred years ago.

He'd have been certain to know my husband
and I'd have been on my way to market to sell the last
of my lettuces. I'd have hopped on to the back of his cart
along with my six children and a goat, which my third youngest
had insisted on bringing. He'd have told me about his five sons,
seven daughters and thirty-nine surviving grandchildren,
one of whom was bound to be called Adam. Then my Cuthbert
would have started singing a popular ballad to his beloved goat,
in time to the steady clop of the hooves of the horse,
and we'd have all joined in, our teeth (untouched by sugar)
sparkling in the fully filtered light.

Eve

As she reached up
to take the fruit
from the tree

did the leaves
brushing her wrist
feel like fingertips

and after she had bitten

did she understand the bruise
on the other side
of the apple

its wound now resting
against the palm
of her hand?

Jessica the criminal

The night she almost became a criminal
she couldn't sleep, so revisited the scene
on foot in the early hours of the morning
with a note containing her insurance details,
to find the car's bumper and what remained
of the wing mirror taped neatly, which she took
to mean her victim was a reasonable person.

Going home she started to worry about
the moisture on the windscreen where she'd left
her confession, remembered rain was expected,
so she returned again with a plastic bag. By 2.30
she was exhausted, from guilt, from walking;
envied the slumbering lawless as she trudged
back up her straight and narrow street.

In my worst moments

when I wondered whether to submit you to a magazine
I imagined myself a grand old lady of poetry
giving what many believed would be my last reading
at a distinguished hall somewhere in London.
I'd start off standing with a chair ready behind me
and there would be a lectern holding all my works
and I'd begin by reading from the period in my writing
that will bear your name in the definitive
biography of my life, from a first edition
of my first collection, which has been promised,
along with the rest of my library and personal papers,
to a university which I once attended. Suddenly,
out of the corner of my eye through a cataract,
I'd notice another old woman rising from the front row
and she would totter up the stairs to the stage and advance
on me, pushing a walking stick into my chest,
demand *Leave my brother* or possibly *husband alone*
you lunatic and send me toppling into the arms
of the great new hope of British poetry who had
been asked to introduce me following an interview
in a broadsheet where he named me his principal influence.
Or maybe afterwards, signing copies of my books
in the foyer, you would shuffle up and rasp
What is the meaning of this you lunatic as you threw
the weighty volume that was my Collected Poems
on to the table. After you'd reminded me exactly
who you were, I could explain, if I'm able to remember,
that back at the turn of the century I'd suffered
from both you and poetry like a disease, but I won't.
So in the face of my silence you will grab me

by the throat of my high-necked blouse with your
liver-spotted hands and the poetry hope, who has been
standing beside me repeating people's names directly
into my ear, will have to intervene. Either way
I will end up in hospital being given a check-up
because of my frailty but my niece or nephew,
or maybe my son or daughter, will notice my face
more animated than it has been for decades
as he or she straps me into their car to take me back
to the Hampstead flat I refuse to give up and I will laugh
and say *He touched me again after all those years.*

Days of 1172

Standing below
my open window
reciting his poems,
they named him a Skald.
Sent him to the castle
to entertain the King.

Standing below
his empty window
reciting my poems,
they called me a Scold.
Took me to the river
to cool off.

Capital cities

In capital cities Jessica Elton
has been known to become despondent
if confronted with tacky merchandise
aimed at tourists. She couldn't tell you
if it's the thought of somebody operating a machine
to make the stuff, the thought of somebody buying it
to thank somebody else for looking after
their pet, or the fact that when she was eight
she thought such things were beautiful.

At a conference in Washington D.C.
not even a sheep farmer from Idaho
and three Bloody Marys from the mini-bar
could console her.

Dans le Cabinet de Toilette, 1907

I'm looking at one of Bonnard's standing nudes
thinking again how much I like his paintings
when my companion for the exhibition returns to my side,

having finished already, not feeling compelled
to read every single caption, and asks me
Why is she wearing a pair of high-heeled shoes

in the bathroom? It's true, she's wearing court shoes
which I hadn't noticed. She's naked, drying herself
with a luminous towel, wearing sunset-coloured shoes

and we find another Bonnard nude on another wall
where she's wearing what could be black slippers
but why would they be pointed? This caption says

it's his wife, and I remember reading in a catalogue
about Bonnard's wife being obsessed with cleanliness,
how she was always washing herself, so Bonnard

was always painting her naked in the bathroom
but she must have had issues about the soles of her feet
touching floor tiles. My date has no such problem.

He tells me he loves going barefoot and he couldn't own
these paintings, those shoes are making him uncomfortable,
and I like Bonnard even more for letting his wife

keep her shoes on and for painting them there.

Handyman

Ideally, he will be a handyman. A strong-tea-drinking,
red-meat-eating man, who can taste the difference
between brake fluid and anti-freeze. A time-keeping,
manual-reading man, who owns one suit. Who knows
how to stroke a dog, stoke a fire, hold a pint.
And on days like these when water leaks, he'll take
my head in his hands and say nothing has happened here
that cannot be set straight by a spirit level, that cannot
be eased back into place by the sole of this sturdy boot.

Jessica Elton's cup of tea

is weak and milky
artificially sweetened
lukewarm by the time
she remembers to drink

so be thankful
you are not it.

Mac

Eating in Regent's Park, the last time that I saw him,
I went to find the toilet and when I came back he was wearing
one of those serious outdoor pursuit macs, carried in his bag
ready for the rain, and I was amazed it fitted in there
but did not say, just zipped up my shower proof jacket
and hoped it wouldn't put me to shame, which it didn't.
But three months later, standing in another park, listening
and trying to see Radiohead, close to a man who had
the same sort of coat as his, and a wedding ring and a wife
who let her husband stand behind her back with his hands
in the pockets of her mac, it did. And soaked to my skin
walking back to the car, I decided I was going to get myself
a mac and a man like that, who would stand and hold me
by its pockets, and I wouldn't get wet like this again.

Second wives

Your love did not find us vertical
and rotating around a dance hall,
or chaperoned on an afternoon lawn

pretending to read. We earned it
like our money, angled over desks,
over your children, comforted you

down corridors. And if you never tore
an evening dress we wore, you never
had to bolt the door against us –

while we accepted you maimed,
the family seat razed to the ground;
that book you kept with grass-stained pages.

Jessica Elton's plea

The next time I wake in the night at three
don't let me be counting these same old sheep
of things I didn't do: the offer of a drink
I didn't take, that trip I could've made to Brazil
to visit the girl I used to sit next to in lectures.
Must I go over again not answering that question
in 1998 playing Trivial Pursuit (afraid to look a fool
and hazard Edgar Allan Poe)? Let my alarm
at three a.m. be for things I did: give me a meadow
of fresh born lambs skipping to the slaughter,
the party where I'm the first one on the dance floor.

Thursday

I'm trying to get to work earlier and make
the short walk from Fenchurch Street Station
to the tube at Tower Hill where a guard
is pulling across the gate and commuters
are being evacuated through the gap
and he says it might be closed for ten minutes
half an hour and I think typical walk back
the way I came and on towards Monument
where it's closed again and this guard says
power failure so I walk towards Bank posting
a birthday card to my sister's boyfriend and at
the entrance to Bank it's the same so I phone
my mum who I know will have the radio on
but she says there's nothing on the travel news
you should get a bus to Victoria so I locate
a bus going to Victoria and follow it
to the bus stop and join the crowd that's formed
to wait for the next one and finally it comes
but it's jammed and I watch with admiration
as people with more balls than I'll ever have
leap on through the exit doors until the driver
gets wise and shuts them so I go and find
another bus stop and settle for a bus to Waterloo
with a seat and tell myself I'm not late yet
I'm getting a different view of the city and then
I hear the man behind say explosion and coming
down the stairs a text arrives from my friend
at work asking if I'm ok and so I phone her
and tell her I'm fine and ask her which is the best
bus to catch to Pimlico and then I try my mum

but now she's engaged and I'm standing opposite
the Shell building where my grandma worked
hoping for a 507 and my mum rings and says
it's bad but all my family members are safe
in their offices and I'm not to get on any more
buses so I start walking through the sirens
aiming for the building where my desk is waiting
exactly the way I left it yesterday evening.

Tonight on the streets of New York

Tonight on the streets of New York
it is so cold that if you cried
the tears would freeze on your face
and a stranger might pluck them off
and make you a necklace

and going into a Manhattan bar
when you took off your scarf
the bartender would watch the glass beads
melt around your throat
and pour you a Jack Daniels without asking.

Poetry dreams

Some nights I dream about poetry. Not in poetry
which my friend thought I meant, the characters
speaking in verse, declaiming heroic couplets

which is maybe how you dream if you happen
to be Milton, but rather what I would term
poetry activities. In one dream I came fourth

in a poetry competition and in another I was at
a reading by an up-and-coming poet who accompanied
each poem with a dance routine. I did once have a good

poetry dream: the one where I went into a country pub
and there at a table were all the great women poets.
They didn't invite me to join them but, ordering my pint

at the bar, I got the impression one of them knew
who I was, and in this dream I remember thinking
that that was something, that this was a start.